First World War
and Army of Occupation
War Diary
France, Belgium and Germany

50 DIVISION
149 Infantry Brigade
Border Regiment
5th Battalion
29 July 1914 - 27 December 1915

WO95/2831/3

The Naval & Military Press Ltd
www.nmarchive.com
Published in association with The National Archives

Published by

The Naval & Military Press Ltd

Unit 10 Ridgewood Industrial Park,

Uckfield, East Sussex,

TN22 5QE England

Tel: +44 (0) 1825 749494

www.naval-military-press.com

www.nmarchive.com

This diary has been reprinted in facsimile from the original. Any imperfections are inevitably reproduced and the quality may fall short of modern type and cartographic standards.

© **Crown Copyright**
Images reproduced by permission of The National Archives, London, England, 2015.

Contents

Document type	Place/Title	Date From	Date To
Heading	WO95/2831 5 Battalion Border Regiment May-Dec 1915		
Heading	50th Division 149th Infy Bde 5th Bn Border Regt May-Dec 1915 To 151 Bde 50 Div		
Heading	149th Inf. Bde. 50th Div. Battn. Disembarked Havre From England 26.10.14. (Note: Battn. Was Posted to 149th Inf. Bde. on 5th May, 1915, having Previously Been On L. Of C.) 1/5th Battn. The Border Regiment. July 1914 to May 1915 (29.7.14 to 28.5.15)		
War Diary	Workington	29/07/1914	29/07/1914
War Diary	Cochermouth	30/07/1914	30/07/1914
War Diary	Workington	04/08/1914	05/08/1914
War Diary	Barrow	14/09/1914	25/10/1914
War Diary	Havre	26/10/1914	04/04/1915
War Diary	Arques	05/04/1915	05/04/1915
War Diary	Droglandt.	05/05/1915	05/05/1915
War Diary	Brandhoek	11/05/1915	12/05/1915
War Diary	Between Vlamertinghe And Ypres	13/05/1915	13/05/1915
War Diary	Hutments about 1 Mile W. of Ypres	14/05/1915	14/05/1915
War Diary	Flamertinghe	16/05/1915	28/05/1915
War Diary	Appendices "A" & "B"		
Miscellaneous	5th Battalion The Border Regt Appendix "A"		
Miscellaneous	5th Bn. The Border Regiment. Roll of Officers Appendix "B"	12/04/1915	12/04/1915
Heading	149th Inf. Bde. 50th Div. 1/5th Battn. The Border Regiment. June (28.5.15-28.6.15) 1915		
War Diary		28/05/1915	28/06/1915
War Diary	149th Inf. Bde. 50th Div. 1/5th Battn. The Border Regiment. July (29.6.15-31.7.15) 1915		
War Diary		29/06/1915	24/07/1915
War Diary	Pont de Nieppe.	24/07/1915	31/07/1915
War Diary			
Heading	149th Inf. Bde. 50th Div. 1/5th Battn. The Border Regiment. August 1915		
War Diary		28/08/1915	01/09/1915
War Diary		01/08/1915	25/08/1915
Heading	149th Inf. Bde. 50th Div. 1/5th Battn. The Border Regiment. September 1915		
War Diary		01/09/1915	30/09/1915
Heading	149th Inf. Bde. 50th Div. 1/5th Battn. The Border Regiment. October 1915		
War Diary		01/10/1915	05/11/1915
Heading	149th Inf. Bde. 50th Div. Battn. transferred to 151st Inf. Bde. 50th Div. 20.12.15 1/5th Battn. The Border Regiment. November And December 1915		
Miscellaneous	D.A.G. 3rd Echelon.	08/03/1916	08/03/1916
War Diary		06/11/1915	27/12/1915
Heading	Appendices "C" & "D"		
Miscellaneous	5th Battalion The Border Regiment. Particulars of Officers.	25/10/1914	25/10/1914

Miscellaneous   Officers Who Have been Granted Have to England
Appendix "D"

(3)

WO95/2831

5 Battalion Border Regiment

May - Dec 1915

50TH DIVISION
149TH INFY BDE

5TH BN BORDER REGT
MAY – DEC 1915

To 151 BDE 50 DIV

149th Inf.Bde.
50th Div.

Battn. disembarked
Havre from England
26.10.14.

(Note: Battn. was
posted to 149th
Inf.Bde. on 5th
May, 1915, having
previously been on
L. of C.)

1/5th BATTN. THE BORDER REGIMENT.

JULY 1914 to MAY 1915

(29.7.14 to 28.5.15)

Attached:

Appendices "A" & "B".

Army Form C. 2118.

WAR DIARY
or
INTELLIGENCE SUMMARY.
(Erase heading not required.)

Instructions regarding War Diaries and Intelligence Summaries are contained in F. S. Regs., Part II. and the Staff Manual respectively. Title pages will be prepared in manuscript.

Hour, Date, Place	Summary of Events and Information	Remarks and References to Appendices
WORKINGTON.		
7-30 p.m. 29th July 1914.	Telegram "MASCOT" received.	
7.0 a.m. 30th July 1914. Cockermouth	Special Service Section left for war station BARROW.	
6-0 p.m. 4th August 1914. Workington	Order to mobilise received.	
6-0 p.m. 5th August 1914. " "	Battalion left for war station BARROW.	
14th September 1914. Barrow.	Orders received to hold 5th Border Regmt in readiness to proceed to the Continent.	
3 p.m. 23rd Oct. 1914. Barrow.	Wire received to hold 5th Border Regt in readiness to embark.	
10-30 p.m. 25th Octr 1914.	Embarked at Southampton on S.S. Manchester Engineer.	
4 p.m. 26th October 1914. HAVRE.	Disembarked at Havre and proceeded to No.1 Rest Camp.	
4 p.m. 27th Octr 1914. HAVRE.	Lieut. RICE and 40 men of "F" Company proceeded to England escorting German prisoners.	
	Captain SOULSBY, Capt SPEDDING, Lieut ASKEW, and 120 other ranks of "F" and "C" Coys proceeded to Genl H.Q. (St. OMER) to conduct German prisoners to HAVRE.	
	"B" and "E" Companies under Capts A.F.BROADLEY-SMITH proceeded to LE MANS.	
... Oct.a 1914 HAVRE.	"H" Company under Captain A.B.COCKBURN proceeded to ROUEN.	

Forms/C. 2118/11.

Army Form C. 2118.

WAR DIARY
or
INTELLIGENCE SUMMARY.
(Erase heading not required.)

Instructions regarding War Diaries and Intelligence
Summaries are contained in F. S. Regs., Part II.
and the Staff Manual respectively. Title pages
will be prepared in manuscript.

Hour, Date, Place	Summary of Events and Information	Remarks and References to Appendices
4 p.m. 28 October 1914. HAVRE.	"A" Company under Captain R.R.BLAIR proceeded to NANTES	
4.10 p.m. 1914 HAVRE	"D" and "E" Companies under CAPT. RIGG and FOTT to the 7 Corps	
7 a.m. October 1914.	4 Officers and 100 men of "D" and "E" companies proceeded to HÉBÉVILLE.	
7.30 p.m. 1 November 1914.	2 Officers and 104 other ranks "D" and "E" companies proceeded to England to escort German prisoners of war under MAJOR A.C. SLOULAR.	
N? November 1914	Headquarters of Battalion moved from Hôtel Camp to RUE RASPAIL, HAVRE. Since arrival at HAVRE the chief duties assigned to the Battalion have been escorting prisoners of war and fatigue guards etc. Owing to the unwillingness of the Cumberland & Westmorland Association T.F. the Battalion proceeds abroad subscribed but the efforts made by the Battalion itself rendered this a great solace. For a fatigue guard it would be a use for the County Association to issue clothing boots & instead of	

(9 29 6) W 2731 100,000 8/14 H W V Forms/C. 2118/11.

WAR DIARY
or
INTELLIGENCE SUMMARY.

(Erase heading not required.)

Army Form C. 2118.

5 Border Regt

14 9/50

Instructions regarding War Diaries and Intelligence Summaries are contained in F. S. Regs., Part II. and the Staff Manual respectively. Title pages will be prepared in manuscript.

Hour, Date, Place	Summary of Events and Information	Remarks and References to Appendices
	trying to board money.	
	The Battalion proceeded abroad 30 officers * and 878 other ranks strong. The great majority were inoculated before proceeding. So far with the exception of a few wet days the weather has been good but cold.	* See app A for note.
20th March 1915.	Received orders on March 20th that this Battalion was to be relieved on the lines of communication by the 1st Cheshire Regt and that we were to concentrate at ARQUES about 2 miles S. of ST. OMER.	
	Present situation of Battalion:-	
	1 Coy. HAVRE — old E & C Coys	
	1 " ROUEN — old A & H Coys	
	1 " BOULOGNE — " D & F "	
	2 platoons ABBEVILLE — " B Coy.	
	2 " DIEPPE — " G Coy.	
	The Battalion assumed the 4 Company system as from	

Forms/C. 2118/11.

149.

Army Form C. 2118.

5" Border Regt-

WAR DIARY
or
INTELLIGENCE SUMMARY.
(Erase heading not required.)

Instructions regarding War Diaries and Intelligence Summaries are contained in F. S. Regs., Part II. and the Staff Manual respectively. Title pages will be prepared in manuscript.

Hour, Date, Place	Summary of Events and Information	Remarks and References to Appendices
	Up to now the duties of the Battalion have been fatigues, guards escorts. We have escorted upwards of 2,000 German prisoners to England.	
9 am April 4th 1915	Headquarters and 1 company left HAVRE for ARQUES. The whole Battalion less the detachment from DIEPPE left	
ARQUES April 5th	arrived at 3 O.M. on April 5th. The Battalion has gone into training. Strength of Battalion is now 30 Officers, 973 other ranks. Lt. M. J. Ingles R.A.M.C. is attached vice Lieut. Bradley been ordered to England. The Chaplain also has gone to England. Major A.C. Lowder was invalided home towards end of march.	
5th May 1915 DROG-ANDT	The Battalion after completing one months training proceeded to its place to take its formation in the Northumberland Brigade Northumbrian Division. Proceeded from ARQUES to DROG-ANDT. Before leaving ARQUES, General STOPFORD, G.O.C. G.H.Q. Troops.	

5th Border

WAR DIARY
or
INTELLIGENCE SUMMARY.
(Erase heading not required.)

Army Form C. 2118.

Instructions regarding War Diaries and Intelligence Summaries are contained in F. S. Regs., Part II. and the Staff Manual respectively. Title pages will be prepared in manuscript.

Hour, Date, Place	Summary of Events and Information	Remarks and References to Appendices
1915.		
BRANDHOEK. May 11th	expressed his pleasure at the efficiency and good conduct of the Battalion. When on the lines of communication good reports were received by the O.C. as to the work done by the various detachments. At Longpré 4 Pte McGhie sent to hospital from ARQUES.	
BRANDHOEK. May 12th	Proceeded here by motor bus yesterday. Evidently in support of French troops. Bivouaced in a wood - glorious weather. 150 men drawn from each Company proceeded at dusk to the west of YPRES on fatigue (filling sandbags and forming barbed wire entanglement). First time under shell fire and no casualties. Returned early next morning.	
BETWEEN VLAMERTINGHE and YPRES 13th May.	The Brigade marched to this place this morning and bivouaced in a field. Bugles were commenced on a journey train. At 5pm order came to move into huts about a mile WEST of YPRES.	

Army Form C. 2118.

WAR DIARY
or
INTELLIGENCE SUMMARY.
(Erase heading not required.)

Instructions regarding War Diaries and Intelligence Summaries are contained in F. S. Regs., Part II. and the Staff Manual respectively. Title pages will be prepared in manuscript.

Hour, Date, Place	Summary of Events and Information	Remarks and References to Appendices
1915.		
Hutments about 1 mile W. of YPRES.	Battalion made dugouts in field behind huts	
14. May	Following is copy of operation order received about 5 p.m.	
	"Operation order No. 15	
	by Brig. Gen. G. P. Feilding, D.S.O. Commanding 149th Bde. Bde H.Q. 14-5-15.	
	1. The Brigade has been placed under the Orders of the 4th Division.	
	2. Battalions have been attached to Brigades of 4th Division	
	as under:—	
	6th N.F. to 11th Bde. 5th Border Regt. to 10th Bde.	
	7th N.F. to 12th Bde.	
	These three Battalions have already joined their respective	
	Brigades and instructions issued to them. They will remain there	
	until to the moral dump to-morrow.	
	3. The 4th and 5th N.F. are placed in Brigade Reserve under	
	the orders of Brig. Gen. Feilding, D.S.O. and will remain in the	
	present position.	
	(Sd.) J. P. Moore, Capt. & Adjutant	
	149 Bde.	
	Companies have been allotted to units of the 10th Inf. Bde.	

WAR DIARY
or
INTELLIGENCE SUMMARY.
(Erase heading not required.)

Army Form C. 2118.

Hour, Date, Place	Summary of Events and Information	Remarks and References to Appendices
1915.	as under:	
FLAMERTINGHE. 16th May.	"A" Coy – Royal Irish Fusiliers – "B" Coy 4 B N H.R. to 1st Royal Warwicks Regt.	
	"B" " – Seaforth Highlanders – "D" " 7th Bn Argyll & Sutherland Highlanders	
17th May.	"C" & "D" Coys proceeded to the trenches the night.	
	"A" & "B" Coys proceeded to the trenches the next night.	
	The 10th Infantry Brigade occupied trenches on the left and right of the St JEAN – ST JULIEN road near St JEAN and	
	1A. BRIQUE. N.E. OF YPRES.	
11 a.m. 24th May 1915.	Enemy attacked with poisonous gas. Attack repulsed but we suffered heavy losses on account of gas.	
	Difficulty was experienced in accounting for casualties owing to the Battalion being split up.	
	2nd Lieut. C. Graham killed in action.	
27th May.		
28th May.	Batt. in trenches. Received order at HOSPITAL FARM near WIMERTINGHE.	

Army Form C. 2118.

WAR DIARY
or
INTELLIGENCE SUMMARY.
(Erase heading not required.)

Instructions regarding War Diaries and Intelligence Summaries are contained in F. S. Regs., Part II. and the Staff Manual respectively. Title pages will be prepared in manuscript.

Hour, Date, Place	Summary of Events and Information	Remarks and References to Appendices
1916		
28th May	Casualties for period 11th to 28th May as under:—	
	KILLED. 0 - 62	
	WOUNDED. 1 - 18.	
	GAS POISON. 3 - 113.	
	MISSING. 90. (see the missing report on a	
	SICK WASTAGE. 48. [been accounted for.	
	2 36	
	6 - 305.	

T./134. Wt. W708—776. 500000. 4/15. Sir J. C. & S.

APPENDICES "A" & "B".

APPENDIX "A"

5th Battalion The Border Regt.
Nominal roll of Officers who proceeded abroad with the Battalion

Lieut. Colonel F. A. Milburn.
Major   A. C. Scoular.
Captain   A. G. Soulsby.
Captain   A. F. Broadley-Smith
Captain   H. J. Bewlay
Captain   R. R. Blair
Captain   A. B. Cowburn.
Captain   S. Rigg.
Captain   W. F. Spedding
Captain   H. R. Potts.
Lieut.   H. C. Webb
Lieut.   J. W. Robinson
Lieut.   W. Adair
Lieut.   E. A. Iredale.
Lieut.   W. S. Sewell
Lieut.   R. J. Rice
Lieut.   F. B. Spedding
Lieut.   C. N. Jenkins
Lieut.   F. P. Longmire
Lieut.   C. Graham
Lieut.   G. G. Askew
Lieut.   J. M. Fanks
Lieut.   H. P. Smith
Lieut.   J. B. McGhie
Lieut.   J. H. M. Humphreys
Lieut.   P. W. Maclagan
Lieut.   W. Marley Cass R.A.M.C.
Capt. & Adjutant   C. W. MacDonald
Major & Quartermaster   F. Picker
Chaplain & Honorary Lieut. Canon Campbell

APPENDIX "B"

5th Bn. The Border Regiment
Roll of Officers

ARQUES.   12-4-16.

Lieut- Colonel J. A. Milburn
Major   A. D. Soulsby
Captain   A. F. Broadley-Smith
   "   H. J. Bewlay
   "   A. B. Cowburn
   "   R. R. Blair
   "   S. Rigg
   "   W. F. Spedding
   "   A. R. Potts
   "   E. A. Iredale
Lieutenant   H. C. Webb
   "   J. W. Robinson
   "   W. Adair
   "   W. S. Sewell
   "   R. J. Rice
   "   F. P. Longmire
   "   C. W. Jenkins
   "   F. B. Spedding
Lieutenant   C. Graham
   "   G. G. Askew
   "   J. N. Franks
   "   H. P. Smith
   "   I. H. M. Humphreys
   "   J. B. McGhie
   "   P. W. Maclagan
   "   J. W. Adair
   "   W. F. D. de La Touche

Captain & Adjutant   J. W. MacDonald
Major & Quartermaster G. Parker
Lieut. M. P. Inglis   R.A.M.C.

149th Inf.Bde.
50th Div.

1/5th BATTN. THE BORDER REGIMENT.

J U N E

(28.5.15-28.6.15)

1 9 1 5

Army Form C. 2118.

WAR DIARY
or
INTELLIGENCE SUMMARY.
(Erase heading not required.)

1/5 Border Regt.

Title pages **June 1915**

Instructions regarding War Diaries and Intelligence Summaries are contained in F. S. Regs., Part II. and the Staff Manual respectively. Title pages will be prepared in manuscript.

Place	Date	Hour	Summary of Events and Information	Remarks and references to Appendices
	May 28th to June 10th		Resting. Usual routine work carried out. The Brigade moved to BUSSEBOOM district during the period.	
	11th June 1915		The Battalion proceeded to the trenches this night. Allotment:- "A"Coy, 41 men of "B"Coy and 25 men of "B"Coy to trench 59 under Capt R.R.Bain. Remainder of Battalion into HOOGE defenses. While in these trenches severe fighting took place. Major A.F. BROADLEY-SMITH was killed, and Capt & Capt T.W. MACDONALD were wounded.	
	16th June	4.15 a.m.	The artillery bombarded the enemy's line from 2-Dm Lee the 3rd Division then attacked. The 14th Bde	

Forms/C. 2118/11.

T/134. Wt. W708—776. 500000. 4/15. Sir J. C. & S.

Army Form C. 2118.

WAR DIARY
or
INTELLIGENCE SUMMARY.
(Erase heading not required.)

Hour, Date, Place	Summary of Events and Information	Remarks and References to Appendices
1915		
11th June	were to seize an opportunity to take the offensive and recapture the position about HOOGE. The attack was unsuccessful. While in these trenches an officer & a corporal of R.E. had occasion to proceed across some open ground in rear of our lines, when the enemy opened machine gun fire on them. The Officer was killed & the Corporal wounded. Capt. R.R.Blair and No 11194 Pte. C. Throssop. "A" Coy went out and brought them under cover of 200 yards, though exposed to the enemy's fire. Battalion relieved and withdrawn into bivouac in SANCTUARY WOOD.	Appendix "C" shows casualties to date for... Appendix "D" shows names Officers granted leave to date & on... Casualties while in HOOGE 11th-16th June 1915:- Killed. O. 1 W. 2 Died of wounds. Other ranks Wounded 2 31
16th June		
17th June	Battalion placed under 151st Brigade in bivouacs. Reserve, and withdrawn to about 1½ miles west of YPRES	
19th June	Battalion withdrawn to billets WEST of VLAMERTINGHE	
20th June	Moved into billets to DRANOUTRE	
21st June	Moved and joined 149th Brigade near NEUVE EGLISE	

WAR DIARY
or
INTELLIGENCE SUMMARY.
(Erase heading not required.)

Army Form C. 2118.

Hour, Date, Place	Summary of Events and Information	Remarks and References to Appendices
1915.		
2	50th Division to join 2nd Army Corps. G.O.C. Officer Comm'dg 2nd Corps addressed 5th Border & 6th N.F.	
21st June	Battalion proceeded to the trenches this night. Quiet period and much work was done improving trenches & wire etc. from protection against shellfire	Casualties 21/6 – 26th June killed 3 wounded 2 bombed 6
26th June	Relieved by 5th D.L.I	

149th Inf.Bde.
50th Div.

1/5th BATTN. THE BORDER REGIMENT.

J U L Y
(29.6.15 - 31.7.15)

1 9 1 5

Attached:

Appendix "E".

Army Form C. 2118.

WAR DIARY
or
INTELLIGENCE SUMMARY.
(Erase heading not required.)

1/5 Border Regt.

July 1915

Instructions regarding War Diaries and Intelligence Summaries are contained in F.S. Regs., Part II. and the Staff Manual respectively. Title pages will be prepared in manuscript.

Place	Date	Hour	Summary of Events and Information	Remarks and references to Appendices
	29th June to 1st July.		In hutments at BULFORD CAMP, near NEUVE EGLISE. The usual routine work carried out.	
	2nd July.	10	Battalion proceeded to the trenches this night. Headquarters ST QUENTINS CABERET, WULVERGHEM.	
	3rd July.		Lieut. R.J. Rice wounded.	
	6th July.		2nd Lieut. E.L. Askew wounded this occurred through a suspicious rifle which was being loaded & put in the frame unexpectedly going off.	
	6th July.		Relieved & proceeded to BULFORD CAMP.	

(9 29 6) W 2794 103,000 8/11 H W V Forms/C. 2118/11.

T/134. Wt. W708—776. 50000. 4/15. Sir J.C.&S.

Army Form C. 2118.

WAR DIARY
or
INTELLIGENCE SUMMARY.
(Erase heading not required.)

Instructions regarding War Diaries and Intelligence Summaries are contained in F. S. Regs, Part II. and the Staff Manual respectively. Title pages will be prepared in manuscript.

Hour, Date, Place	Summary of Events and Information	Remarks and References to Appendices
1915		
7th July	A board of officers composed as under assembled at Bulford Camp, to report upon the circumstances attending the deficiency of 400 odd emergency rations issued to the N.C.Os and men of the Battalion:-	
	President - Captain S. Rigg.	
	Members - Lieut. C.N. Jenkins.	
	2/Lt. J.N. Franks.	
	The following intended to attend QMS and all CQMSs, 1 N.CO. and 1 man per Coy.	
7th July to 10th July	Finding sent to Bde H.Q.	
10th July	"Usual routine" work carried out.	
	The Battalion proceeded to the trenches this night. Headquarters ST QUENTIN'S CABARET, WULVERGHEM.	
11th July	The undermentioned officers joined from 2/5th Bn Border Regt and posted to Companies as under:-	
	Capt. R.C. Lockett. "D" 2/Lt. W.P. Bennett "B"	

WAR DIARY
or
INTELLIGENCE SUMMARY.
(Erase heading not required.)

Army Form C. 2118.

Hour, Date, Place	Summary of Events and Information	Remarks and References to Appendices
1915		
	Lieut. H. Bennett "C" 2/Lt H. E. Wood "B"	
	Lieut. P.B.C. Holdsworth "A" Lt. A.L. Wilson "C"	
	2/Lt. C.A. Montgomery "A" 2/Lt. F.B. Clarke "C"	
	2/Lt. Harman "B" Lt. R.B. Glass "D"	
	2/Lt. O.F. Feedan "C" 2/Lt. J.R. Percy "D"	
	Capt. Rigg transferred from D Coy to command of B	
	Company. Capt. Noxele to command D Coy.	
13th July	Lieut. R.W. Marley having been detained at ROUEN	
14th July	joined the Battalion and posted to D Coy.	
1st	Lieut. P.B.C. Holdsworth wounded. Capt. R.B. Clair to hospital.	
	Battalion relieved by 2nd Canadian Battn & proceeded to	
	ALDERSHOT CAMP.	
16th July	The Brigade marched to ARMENTIÈRES. 5th B "Border Regt."	
	took over trenches 74 and 75. and their supports from the	
	4th Br R. fr. B de.	
17th July	2/Lt. J.R. Percy wounded.	

Army Form C. 2118.

WAR DIARY
or
INTELLIGENCE SUMMARY.
(Erase heading not required.)

Instructions regarding War Diaries and Intelligence Summaries are contained in F. S. Regs., Part II. and the Staff Manual respectively. Title pages will be prepared in manuscript.

Hour, Date, Place	Summary of Events and Information	Remarks and References to Appendices
1915.		
18th July	Lieut H Bennett to hospital.	
20th July	An Hellcom relieved by 7th N.F. Proceeded to the ASYLUM.	
	ARMENTIERES	
20th July to 24th July	In Brigade reserve.	
24th July PONT de NIEPPE	In Brigade moved to tents at PONT de NIEPPE near	
28th July		
29th July	Major Lese went on 1/8/15.	
30th July	Lieut Colonel J.A. McBain to England on sick leave.	
30th July	2c J.N. FRANKE to hospital.	
31st July	9e R.W. MARLEY to hospital.	

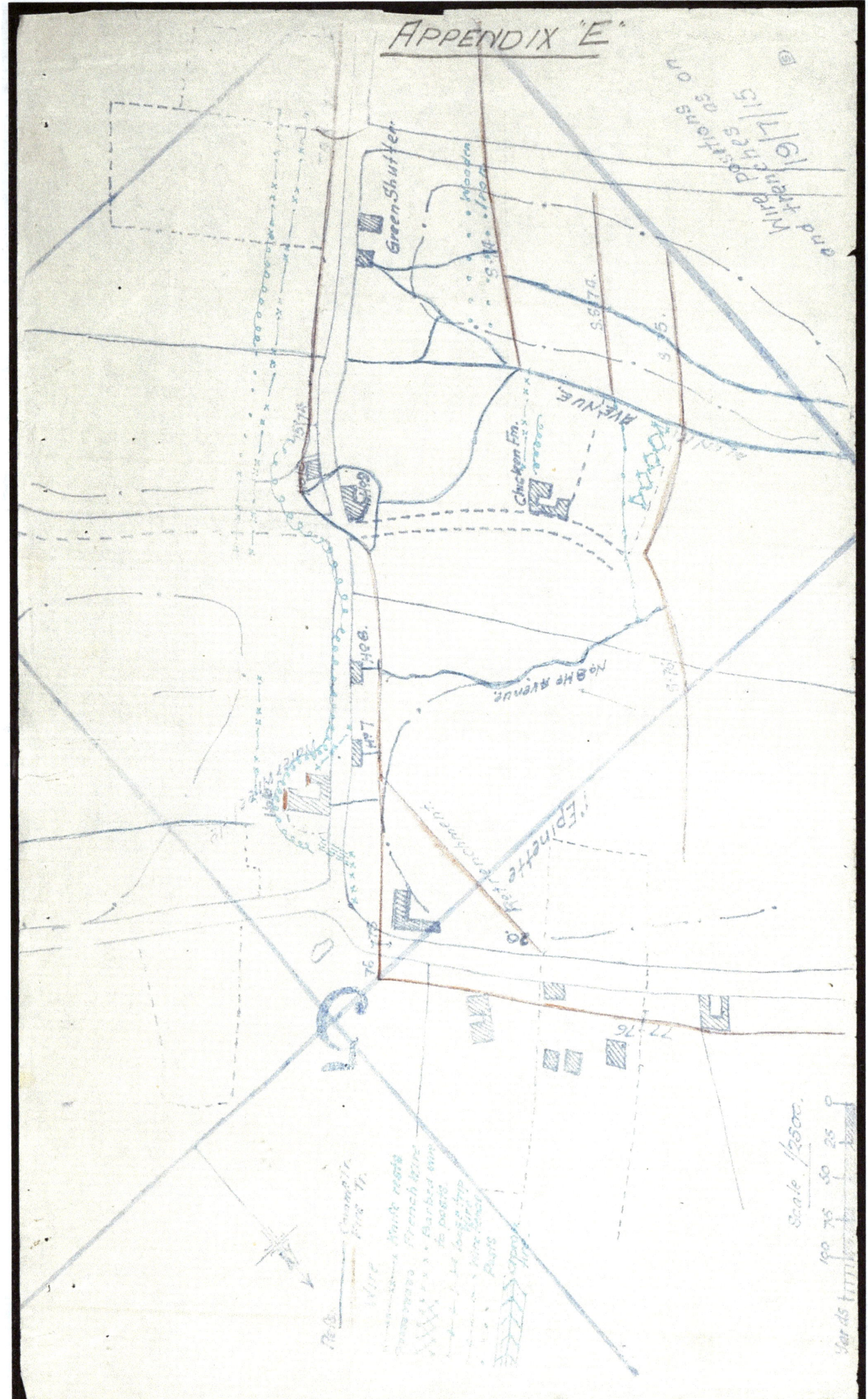

149th Inf.Bde.
50th Div.

1/5th BATTN. THE BORDER REGIMENT.

A U G U S T

1 9 1 5

Army Form C. 2118.

WAR DIARY
or
INTELLIGENCE SUMMARY.
(Erase heading not required.)

Instructions regarding War Diaries and Intelligence Summaries are contained in F. S. Regs., Part II. and the Staff Manual respectively. Title pages will be prepared in manuscript.

Hour, Date, Place	Summary of Events and Information	Remarks and References to Appendices
1915.		
11 a.m. 28th August 1915.	Redoubt about 5 p.m. Enemy replied with 16 French bombs. No casualties.	
	Nothing out of the ordinary has happened. About 6.15 p.m. on the 27th shot an enemy aeroplane flew directly towards our trenches at about 500 yards elevation. Our men opened fire & it at once turned and flew back.	
11 a.m. 30th August.	The usual patrols & working parties were out. Sentries reported tapping to be heard near a house 6 (see app. F) A bore was put down & reached water. O.C. Trench 7 reports that German patrols are in the habit of crawling up the ditch continuation of PANH AVENUE with towards the German lines) and firing flares to our line. German snipers have smashed 3 of our periscopes.	
The day of 31st Aug / 1st Sept.	Battalion relieved by the 5th Yorks and marched to billets at HOSPICE CIVILE, ARDENTIERES.	

Army Form C. 2118.

WAR DIARY
or
INTELLIGENCE SUMMARY.

1/5 Border Regt.

August 1915

(Erase heading not required.)

Place	Date	Hour	Summary of Events and Information	Remarks and references to Appendices
	1st August.		The Battalion proceeded to the trenches. H.Q. to HAYSTACK FARM near CHAPELLE D'ARMENTIERES.	
	13th August.		Lieut. G.B. Spedding to hospital.	
	15th August 1915.		Battalion relieved & passed into HOSPICE CIVILE, ARMENTIERES. Capt. W.G. Spedding appointed from 3/5 Bn the Border Regt. Brought up 40 other ranks from the base.	
	18th August.		Capt. F.R. Grice rejoined from R. Gen Base Depot, ROUEN.	

Army Form C. 2118.

WAR DIARY
or
INTELLIGENCE SUMMARY.
(Erase heading not required.)

Instructions regarding War Diaries and Intelligence Summaries are contained in F. S. Regs., Part II. and the Staff Manual respectively. Title pages will be prepared in manuscript.

Hour, Date, Place	Summary of Events and Information	Remarks and References to Appendices
1915. 19th August	The Battalion moved into the ASYLUM in Brigade Reserve.	
21st August.	Draft of 109 other ranks joined from 9/6th Border Regt.	
23rd August.	Battalion relieved 7th N.F. in the trenches at PLANK AVENUE. Trenches taken over at Plank Avenue are shown in Sketch map. APPENDIX I.V.E. which is enlarged from map. BELGIUM and FRANCE ("B" Series) Sheet 36. (4th Edn) The Battalion occupied these trenches from July 16th to 20th. The map shows the trenches at that time.	
11 a.m. 24th August.	Quiet night except for enemys machine gun fire. Thick fog prevailed. Past 24 hours generally quiet.	
11 a.m. 25th August.	Trench 7th dispersed an enemy working party. Officer's patrol from Trench 7H between 11.30 a.m. and 1 a.m. reports enemy busy putting sandbags on BLACK REDOUBT. Our Trench Howitzers opened fire on the enemys Black	

149th Inf.Bde.
50th Div.

1/5th BATTN. THE BORDER REGIMENT.

S E P T E M B E R

1 9 1 5

Army Form C. 2118.

WAR DIARY
or
INTELLIGENCE SUMMARY.
(Erase heading not required.)

Instructions regarding War Diaries and Intelligence Summaries are contained in F. S. Regs., Part II. and the Staff Manual respectively. Title pages will be prepared in manuscript.

Hour, Date, Place	Summary of Events and Information	Remarks and References to Appendices
1st Sept. 1915.	Resumption of duties. Blank by indicates rank of officer.	
	Approved by Divisional Commander:-	
	Present rank name rank approved	
	Major A.D. Bulsby Lieut-Colonel	
	Captain A.J. Bentley Major	
	2/Lt W.P. Bennett Lieutenant	
	2/Lt R.B. Mabel Lieutenant	
	2/Lt A.E. Wood Lieutenant	
2nd September	No 2113 Pte/Cpl C. Ex PASS, D Coy commenced as Lieut to the 2/5th Border Regt.	
	The usual routine work has been carried out while resting.	
6/7th September	The Battn relieved the 6th Bn D.L.I. in Trenches 68 and 69 and their supports & close supports near CHAPELLE D'ARMENTIERES.	
11 a.m. 7th September	Patrol from Trench 69 heard enemy transport at 12·15 a.m. at 1·17 & 3·0. Trap 36 Belgium & France. at 1·30 a.m.	

WAR DIARY
or
INTELLIGENCE SUMMARY.
(Erase heading not required.)

Army Form C. 2118.

Instructions regarding War Diaries and Intelligence Summaries are contained in F. S. Regs., Part II. and the Staff Manual respectively. Title pages will be prepared in manuscript.

Hour, Date, Place	Summary of Events and Information	Remarks and References to Appendices
1915		
11am 6th Septr.	Enemy searchlights were on both flanks. Patrol under Capt. Blair from trench 68 got close to German line. There seemed to be little if any work going on & the Germans could be heard whistling, talking and singing. Trench 69 reports night quiet, and no movement on part of enemy. Our own wire was patrolled and weak places noted.	
11am 9th Septr.	Trench 68 reports enemy working party on side their own wire. The patrol could not get near the enemy line on account of the noise made by moving through the corn, which drew fire. A German working party was heard opposite trench 69 last night. Our machine Gun opens fire but the enemy resumed work after a very brief pause. A horse and light cart was heard by our patrol	

Army Form C. 2118.

WAR DIARY
or
INTELLIGENCE SUMMARY.
(Erase heading not required.)

Instructions regarding War Diaries and Intelligence Summaries are contained in F. S. Regs., Part II. and the Staff Manual respectively. Title pages will be prepared in manuscript.

Hour, Date, Place	Summary of Events and Information	Remarks and References to Appendices
1915.		
Mon. 10th September	very close to the enemy's front-line. At 11 a.m. the enemy began to send "Whezz-bangs" over. Capt. Loebb observed position of flashes from enemy guns & informed F.O.O. Position of one enemy gun was I-23-B-8-7 (Map 3c Belgium & France) after this battery had been fired on by our guns no more artillery activity on part of enemy during that day. At 3.10 p.m. GER incl: two pigeons were observed flying over trench 68 towards German lines.	
Mon. 11th September	German working party observed opposite the centre of trench log at 11 p.m. yesterday. Machine gun fire was opened & the party dispersed.	
Mon. 12th September	In the morning the enemy fired 10 shells into fire trench 68. No casualties as men were moved. Our patrol from trench 68 came from 8.30 p.m. 11.6. 1.30 a.m. 12th inst. 100 yards of German trenches	

WAR DIARY
or
INTELLIGENCE SUMMARY.
(Erase heading not required.)

Army Form C. 2118.

Hour, Date, Place	Summary of Events and Information	Remarks and References to Appendices
1915.		
13th September.	No patrols or working parties left their lines during this time. A patrol from trench 69 about 8pm to 10.30pm got got within 25 yards of the German trench. Germans searchlight began to play on their own parapet and there an excellent view of the enemy's line was obtained. The German wire was in a very good state and behind the wire was a forward trench in front of the parapet. Last night Captain Blair went out with a patrol from trench 68. He got right up to the German wire and was able to cut a piece off it. This was sent to Brigade Headquarters with an excellent sketch of the area by Capt. Blair. Officers patrols from trench 69 about 250 yards forward but were unable to discover any signs of enemy activity	
14th September.		

WAR DIARY or INTELLIGENCE SUMMARY.

Army Form C. 2118.

(Erase heading not required.)

Hour, Date, Place	Summary of Events and Information	Remarks and References to Appendices
1915		
Night 14th/15th September	Battalion relieved by 6th & 7th N.F. and Battalion moved to billets in ASYLUM.	
16th September 1915	Fatigue parties as under supplied to 2nd Northumbrian Field Coy. R.E. at S.W. gates of the ASYLUM at 7.15 p.m.:- 1 officer and 35 men with 20 picks and 5 shovels 1 officer and 30 men with 20 picks and 5 shovels	
17th September	The following copy message from 149th Bde begins. Please note that you will find the following working parties tonight. viz (A) 1 officer and 50 men without tools (B) 1 officer and 40 men with 20 shovels and 10 picks (C) 2 officers and 80 men with 60 shovels and 20 picks (D) 1 officer and 25 men with 20 shovels and 5 picks. (E) 1 officer and 20 men with 20 shovels and picks All the above except E will report to 2nd Northumbrian Field Coy R.E. at S.W. gate of the ASYLUM at 7 p.m. Party (E) will report to O.C. 2nd Northumbrian Field Coy RE at	

Army Form C. 2118.

WAR DIARY
or
INTELLIGENCE SUMMARY.
(Erase heading not required.)

Hour, Date, Place	Summary of Events and Information	Remarks and References to Appendices
1915.		
19th September.	LILLE POSTS at 9 a.m. tomorrow on 20.	
20th September.	Battalion moved to rest billets at ARMENTIERES.	
	Following parties to be found tonight:-	
	2 Officers and 150 men to report to O.C. 1st Northumbrian	
	Field Company R.E. at main gate of ASYLUM at 8 p.m.	
	2 Officers and 100 men to report to O.C. 2nd Northumbrian	
	Field Coy R.E. at S.W. gate of the ASYLUM at 7 p.m.	
	Each man of both parties to be provided with a pick	
	and shovel.	
	Battalion inspected by Major General Sir H.C.O. PLUMER.	
	Commanding 2nd Army.	
21st September.	Following working party supplied tonight:- 2 Officers	
	and 200 men to report to Adjt Coopany R.E. at CHURCH	
	ST. VARSTE, ARMENTIERES at 7 p.m. Every man will carry a	
	shovel and 100 of the party will carry picks.	
22nd September.	Major H.R.P. KEMMIS-BETTY, from 5th Service Battalion	

WAR DIARY
or
INTELLIGENCE SUMMARY.
(Erase heading not required.)

Army Form C. 2118.

Hour, Date, Place	Summary of Events and Information	Remarks and References to Appendices
1915.		
23, 24th Sept.	The Royal Berkshire Regiment assumed command of the Battalion from this date. Brigade relieves 151st Brigade in trenches 74 to 80 (inclusive) tonight. Battalion takes over following trenches: from 6th D.L.I. and 5th L.N.L - Trench 75 from House 8 exclusive. Trenches 76 and 77 and their supports and Support Point Y.	
5-26 pm 24th September.	Following from Brigade begins In the event of the issue not being favourable tomorrow morning the bombardment will start at 5 am without the others.	
9:45 pm 24th September.	Following message received through usual channels from G.H.Q begins Chief wishes troops to be informed that he feels confident they will realise how much our success in the forthcoming operations depends upon the individual efforts of each officer N.C.O and man aaa He wishes this to be conveyed to them verbally and in such a manner	See App. E.

WAR DIARY
or
INTELLIGENCE SUMMARY.
(Erase heading not required.)

Army Form C. 2118.

Hour, Date, Place	Summary of Events and Information	Remarks and References to Appendices
1915.		
Hun. to bar. 25th Sepr.	not to disclose our intentions to the enemy and ends "Trench 76 reports everything quiet." A demonstration was organised by the 50th Division as a support to the advance to be commenced north and south. Arrangements were made to produce a smoke with the idea of creating in the mind of the enemy fear of an attack in our sector of gas so causing him to keep his trenches fully manned. At the same time heavy artillery fire was to be opened with machine gun and rapid fire from the trenches. The night of the 24/25th was spent in arranging straw in front of No. 76 and 77 trenches some wet, and that nearer our trenches dry soaked with paraffin. Thielgallite bombs were to be used in front of Trench 76 and this part of the programme was in the hands of Lieut Adair, Battalion Grenadier Officer, in conjunction with No. 2 Sec. Brigade Grenadier	

Army Form C. 2118.

WAR DIARY
or
INTELLIGENCE SUMMARY.
(Erase heading not required.)

Instructions regarding War Diaries and Intelligence Summaries are contained in F. S. Regs., Part II. and the Staff Manual respectively. Title pages will be prepared in manuscript.

Hour, Date, Place	Summary of Events and Information	Remarks and References to Appendices
1915.	Officers. the demonstration was timed to begun at 4-50 a.m. but was postponed one hour on account of the wind. At 6-0 a.m. four minutes after the intended time to commence a message was received from Brigade not to light up. This arrived too late for 77 trench, as their straw had been lighted, the smoke going well over the German lines, about 460 yards distant. The following Officers were in charge of trenches on this occasion:—	
	Trench 75 - Major Bowley — Trench 76 - Capt. Webb.	
	Trench 77 - Capt. Read. — Supports. Capt. Costron	
	M.G. Officers - Lieut. Wood. — Grenadier Officer. Lieut. Adam.	
	In preparing for this demonstration, the straw had to be carried 3/4 of a mile the day before and was laid the whole length of 76 and 77 trenches. Great credit is due to the men for the willing and cheerful way in	

Army Form C. 2118.

WAR DIARY
or
INTELLIGENCE SUMMARY.
(Erase heading not required.)

Instructions regarding War Diaries and Intelligence Summaries are contained in F. S. Regs., Part II. and the Staff Manual respectively. Title pages will be prepared in manuscript.

Hour, Date, Place	Summary of Events and Information	Remarks and References to Appendices
1915.		
25 September	whilst they carried out an arduous piece of work.	
	O.C. Trench 77 reports that a strong bombing patrol from his trench reached about 80 yards from the German line when they were fired upon by the German patrol in listening post. Two bombs were thrown at the place and were answered by shots from the enemy's trenches.	
	O.C. Trench 78 reports enemy replied to rapid fire then opened at 4.50 a.m. with "whizzbangs".	
11.30 a.m. 25th September	Message from Bn. H.Q. asks for arrangements to get all information by patrols or otherwise.	
10.7 p.m. 25th September	Shelling from bivouac begins and utmost activity will be shown during tonight by patrols both to grub enemy and to discover any movements on his part. No raid.	
26 September	Trench 75 reports night quiet. Patrols out continually but nothing to report.	

Army Form C. 2118.

WAR DIARY
or
INTELLIGENCE SUMMARY.
(Erase heading not required.)

Instructions regarding War Diaries and Intelligence Summaries are contained in F. S. Regs, Part II. and the Staff Manual respectively. Title pages will be prepared in manuscript.

Hour, Date, Place	Summary of Events and Information	Remarks and References to Appendices
1915.		
2nd Sept.	Trench 77 reports patrols out but all quiet. Both trenches were fired on by enemy from the trenches.	
	Trench 76 reports patrols out nothing to report.	
	Capt. Cockburn reports enemy fires on the old support beginning	
	at 11.20 a.m. infiltrating from left. No fresh movements and direction not accurately described to be of use. There were	
	heavy cheers and burst accompanied by black smoke.	
3rd September 1915.	At 8.15 p.m. 2nd Captn. R.R.Blair took out a party consisting of the following to examine the enemy wire. Sgt Graham Cpl. Lyffen, L/c Mossop, Pte Hopthrow, Bace, Coles, Walker, Marker, Rooney and Barrah. 7 men were detailed to go to the right to bomb the listening post in the gap, from which previous patrols had been fired on. Captain Blair and 3 others were to creep up to the German wire. This latter party reached a point within about 30 yards of their objective but owing to the amount of talking the Officer considered it unsafe at that time and withdrew to a dit

Army Form C. 2118.

WAR DIARY
or
INTELLIGENCE SUMMARY.
(Erase heading not required.)

Instructions regarding War Diaries and Intelligence Summaries are contained in F. S. Regs., Part II. and the Staff Manual respectively. Title pages will be prepared in manuscript.

Hour, Date, Place	Summary of Events and Information	Remarks and References to Appendices
1915 27th Sep G.	bringing the 7 bombers back to their places, to wait until it was quiet. In the meantime Sgnt. Iffers reported the ditch to be weak across about 60 yards to the right. The N.C.O. with three others was sent along to cut this wire while the remainder of the party waited about 20 minutes after this a German party came past going from their recent H.qrs. Bears lured his men on the edge of the ditch and waited for the enemy patrol which was coming forward about 20 yards at a time. The officer allowed them to get within ten yards of him when he opened fire with his revolver and shot four, including an officer. The remainder of the Germans lay down and our men opened rapid fire. Capt. Bears who was in advance of his men went back to the ditch to reload his revolver	

Army Form C. 2118.

WAR DIARY
or
INTELLIGENCE SUMMARY.
(Erase heading not required.)

Instructions regarding War Diaries and Intelligence Summaries are contained in F. S. Regs., Part II. and the Staff Manual respectively. Title pages will be prepared in manuscript.

Hour, Date, Place	Summary of Events and Information	Remarks and References to Appendices
1915 27th September	Five Germans got up & ran, and our party opened fire. Three fell, but two appeared to get away. Capt. Blair then went forward & examined the body of a German private, which was carried along the ditch into our trench. At 12.30 a.m. the same night Capt Liffen again went out with 3 men and removed various articles including a portrait which was of great value. It is thought that this party was only saved by practically annihilating the German trenches and he was preserved this falsol. Captain Blair and his men performed work of great benefit. O.C. Trench 70 reports enemy baling water out of advanced trench. O.C. Trench 71 reports a new enemy machine gun opposite his trench. Also gives bearing of a gun which	

(9 29 6) W 2734 103,000 8/14 H W V Forms/C. 2118/11.

Army Form C. 2118.

WAR DIARY
or
INTELLIGENCE SUMMARY.
(Erase heading not required.)

Instructions regarding War Diaries and Intelligence Summaries are contained in F. S. Regs., Part II. and the Staff Manual respectively. Title pages will be prepared in manuscript.

Hour, Date, Place	Summary of Events and Information	Remarks and References to Appendices
1915		
27th September	Fired 4 high explosive shells into HOUPLINES.	
	50 "Whizzbangs" were sent into 74, 75, 76 & 77 supports	
	by enemy between 2.15 pm & 3pm. Situation of guns	
	firing reported to F.O.O. Snipers in trench 77 shot 2	
	Germans who were coming out to the bodies of those	
	killed last night.	
28th September	Relief of 75 trench before supports carried out. 75	
	now commanded by Captain Boisbrun & supports by	
	Major Buslay.	
	The enemy's wire appears to consist of two rows of	
	knife rests with 12 trip wire between.	
	No recent enemy's patrol have found copies	
	of the GAZETTE des ARDENNES placed by the enemy in	
	places where they could be easily found.	
29th September	Following received from 18th Div H.Q. being 2nd Corps wire	
	begins G.652 It is particularly important that the	

Army Form C. 2118.

WAR DIARY
or
INTELLIGENCE SUMMARY.
(Erase heading not required.)

Instructions regarding War Diaries and Intelligence
Summaries are contained in F. S. Regs., Part II.
and the Staff Manual respectively. Title pages
will be prepared in manuscript.

(31)

Hour, Date, Place	Summary of Events and Information	Remarks and References to Appendices
1915.		
29 September.	Units should be identified near LEPINETTE and between LE TOCQUET and LE GHEER on R. Please report any information to this Office without delay enB.	
30th September.	O.C. 11 Trench nothing to report. No patrol out on account of very heavy rain. Capt. Webb reports patrol from his Trench (16) Located an enemy listening post. When this could be heard at some interval it was thought that this was the signal for changing the listening party as four men could be seen come to Report and four return. Enemy Whizz Bangers fired 75 at 11.20 p.m. Howitzer Battery replied.	

149th Inf.Bde.
50th Div.

1/5th BATTN. THE BORDER REGIMENT.

O C T O B E R

1 9 1 5

Army Form C. 2118.

WAR DIARY
or
INTELLIGENCE SUMMARY.

1/5 Border Regt.

October 1915

(Erase heading not required.)

Place	Date	Hour	Summary of Events and Information	Remarks and references to Appendices
Potijze			O.C. 2nd L.I. reports German patrol in the detail where their other patrol was annihilated. Is of opinion that the bodies are being left there by the German in the hope of catching our men going out to them.	

Army Form C. 2118.

WAR DIARY
or
INTELLIGENCE SUMMARY.
(Erase heading not required.)

Instructions regarding War Diaries and Intelligence Summaries are contained in F. S. Regs., Part II. and the Staff Manual respectively. Title pages will be prepared in manuscript.

Hour, Date, Place	Summary of Events and Information	Remarks and References to Appendices
1915		
1st October	/5 trench nothing to report. Moon too bright for patrol. O.C. Trench /6 (bomb both) reports our howitzers burst in front of enemys parapet opposite Bay 23. Our machine gun was turned on the gap during the night.	
2nd October	B.T. Trench /1 reports that the enemy fired 20 "whizbangs" into his trench between 11am & 12.30pm yesterday. Part of the parapet blown in but no material damage done. O.C. Trench /10 reports that 3pm yesterday one of enemy's sentries was seen to be belonging a gun. rifle bat. opposite Bay 10. nothing to report. O.C. /1 trench reports everything quiet. A piece of white paper was on a stick near the German bodies. This was shot off by one of our snipers. O.C. /5 trench reports night quiet. Enemys snipers	

Army Form C. 2118.

WAR DIARY
or
INTELLIGENCE SUMMARY.
(Erase heading not required.)

Instructions regarding War Diaries and Intelligence Summaries are contained in F. S. Regs., Part II. and the Staff Manual respectively. Title pages will be prepared in manuscript.

Hour, Date, Place	Summary of Events and Information	Remarks and References to Appendices
1915.		
4th October.	Are heavy and accurate opposite this front. On the night of 4/10/15 clean shirts and socks were received from PONT de NIEPPE baths for the whole Battalion in the trenches.	
5th October.	O.C. 75 Trench Mortars reports nothing special to report, except that enemy's sniping continues particularly accurate. Rifles are fired on parapets by day and accurate shooting takes place at night. O.C. 76 reports enemy very quiet. O.C. 77 do	
6th October.	During the last few days the 8th Bn Loyal North Lancashire Regiment have been attached to the Brigade for instruction. A letter of thanks for the valuable instruction was received by O.C. 149th Bde from O.C. 8th L.N.L. Regt.	
7th October.	Enemy fired about 20 trench mortar shells in the neighbourhood of CHICKEN FARM. No damage was done.	

Army Form C. 2118.

WAR DIARY
or
INTELLIGENCE SUMMARY.
(Erase heading not required.)

Instructions regarding War Diaries and Intelligence Summaries are contained in F. S. Regs., Part II. and the Staff Manual respectively. Title pages will be prepared in manuscript.

Hour, Date, Place	Summary of Events and Information	Remarks and References to Appendices
1915		
7th October	O.C. Trench 75 of opinion that a relief took place on the enemy trenches opposite on the night of the 6th. Trench 71 nothing to report. O.C. Trench 76 reports the enemy heard working at his sap head in front of trench 76 about 11.30 a.m. Earth was observed being thrown out and a sound as of hammering upon metal was also heard. O.C. Trench 75 reports enemy transport heard on road I-12-Central to 75 Central at 8.30 a.m. Afterwards men were seen carrying stores from this road. O.C. Trench 76 reports new machine gun emplacement opposite Bay 13 in his trench.	
8th October	An officers patrol from trench 76 at 9 p.m. reported all quiet. About midnight metal tubs were heard being unloaded in the enemy's line. Patrols from trench 77 at 9 p.m. and 3 a.m. reported all quiet.	

Army Form C. 2118.

WAR DIARY
or
INTELLIGENCE SUMMARY.
(Erase heading not required.)

Hour, Date, Place	Summary of Events and Information	Remarks and References to Appendices
1915.		
9th October	Battn relieved by H & N.F. and 7th and marched to billets in ARMENTIERES.	
11th October	Following working parties supplied to report to O.C. 1st Northumbrian Field Coy. R.E. at the ASYLUM at 6.30pm 1 Officer and 60 men without tools. 2 N.C.O's and 25 men with shovels.	
12th October	Following working parties to report to O.C. 1st Northumbrian Field Company R.E. at the ASYLUM at 6.30 p.m. 1 Officer and 50 men without tools. 2 N.C.O's and 25 men with shovels.	
14th October	The Battalion relieved the 4th and 7th N.F. in the following trenches:- Trench 78. Trench 79. CANADA ROAD. Trench 78 Support. Support Point "Z". and Trench 79 Support "B".	
15th October	Trench 78 nothing to report " 79 do	

Army Form C. 2118.

WAR DIARY
or
INTELLIGENCE SUMMARY.
(Erase heading not required.)

Instructions regarding War Diaries and Intelligence Summaries are contained in F. S. Regs., Part II. and the Staff Manual respectively. Title pages will be prepared in manuscript.

Hour, Date, Place	Summary of Events and Information	Remarks and References to Appendices
1915		
15th October.	Patrols were out from both trenches becoming our wire and front generally.	
16th October.	Trench 78 nothing to report except enemy searchlight at intervals during the night. Trench 79 at 10.30pm 15th 3 hand grenades were thrown at our machine gun which were firing intermittently. All fell short.	
17th October.	Officers patrol out from Trench 79. Nothing to report.	
18th October.	Nothing to report.	
19th October.	The enemy put 8 heavy shells into trench 78 between 11am & 12 noon. 1 man killed & 1 wounded. Trench 79 reports all quiet during the night. In the afternoon the enemy put over 30 rifle grenades all of which fell short.	
20th October.	Trench 78 reports all quiet. Trench 79 do. No enemy in their trench	

WAR DIARY
or
INTELLIGENCE SUMMARY.
(Erase heading not required.)

Army Form C. 2118.

Instructions regarding War Diaries and Intelligence Summaries are contained in F. S. Regs., Part II. and the Staff Manual respectively. Title pages will be prepared in manuscript.

Hour, Date, Place	Summary of Events and Information	Remarks and References to Appendices
1915.		
20th October	report seeing two Germans in helmets.	
21st October	nothing to report.	
	Following message received from 50th Division begins aaa War office telegraph Minister Munitions asks for services of Captain R.R. Blair 5th Border Regt for 3 mon. aaa Temporary extension leave tendered pending decision aaa Any objection? ends. No objections were raised. Capt. Blair proceeds on leave to England 18-10-16.	
22nd October.	Trench 78 nothing to report. Trench 79 reports seeing a German wearing a blue grey cap with a red band round it and two buttons in the middle. The sniper in this trench reports having hit a box which he took for a periscope and immediately 3 pigeons flew from it.	
23rd October.	Patrol from trench 78 were out and nothing to report.	

WAR DIARY
or
INTELLIGENCE SUMMARY.
(Erase heading not required.)

Army Form C. 2118.

Hour, Date, Place	Summary of Events and Information	Remarks and References to Appendices
1915		
23rd October	They brought in an imitation cannon which they found on an upturned cart opposite Bay 25. Trench 79 reports having located an enemy periscope hidden in a rusty iron tin.	
24th October	Trench 78 reports all quiet. Night too light for patrolling. Trench 79 reports having put a bullet through the enemy periscope located yesterday.	
25th October	Battalion relieved by 10th Yorkshire Regiment and marched to billets in ARMENTIERES.	
26th October	The Brigade marched to LA CRECHE and late the night in some barns.	
27th October	Proceeded to STRAZEELE for a period of training and refitting. The Battalion is billeted at different farms.	
28th October	Owing to wet weather not much work has yet been	

Instructions regarding War Diaries and Intelligence Summaries are contained in F.S. Regs., Part II. and the Staff Manual respectively. Title pages will be prepared in manuscript.

WAR DIARY
or
INTELLIGENCE SUMMARY.
(Erase heading not required.)

Army Form C. 2118.

Instructions regarding War Diaries and Intelligence Summaries are contained in F.S. Regs., Part II. and the Staff Manual respectively. Title pages will be prepared in manuscript.

Hour, Date, Place	Summary of Events and Information	Remarks and references to Appendices
1915	done. The following is a summary of the work proposed to be done for week 30-10-15 to 6-11-15.	

Date	time 1st parade	"A" Company	"B" Company	"C" Company	"D" Company	Machine Gun Section	Grenadier Section	Signallers
Oct 30th	7.0am	Physical drill	Physical drill	Physical drill	Physical drill	Under Brigade Arrangements	Under Brigade Arrangements	Physical drill. Instruction in mechanism and action of the rifle (O.R)
	9.30am	Route march	Platoon arms and company drill	Route march	Platoon arms and Company drill			Visual signalling with discs
	2.0pm	Lecture	Gastmounting	Lecture	Guard mounting			
31st	7.0am	Running	Running	Running	Running			Running
	9.30am	Church parade and inspection	Church parade and inspection					
	2.0pm							
1st Nov	7.0am	Physical drill	Bayonet fighting	Bayonet fighting	Bayonet fighting			Physical drill
	9.30am	Platoon arms & Company drill	Route march	Platoon arms and Company drill	Route march			Route march. Practice in laying, aiming, repairing
	2.0pm	Guard mounting parade	Lecture	Lecture	Lecture			
2nd	7.0am	Bayonet exercise	Physical drill	Bayonet drill	Physical drill			Physical drill
	9.30am	Route march	Extended order drill	Route march	Extended order drill			Buzzer practice
	2.0pm	Arms drill under Battalion Sergeant Major						Co-op. Lamp practice

Army Form C. 2118.

WAR DIARY
or
INTELLIGENCE SUMMARY.

(Erase heading not required.)

Instructions regarding War Diaries and Intelligence Summaries are contained in F. S. Regs., Part II. and the Staff Manual respectively. Title pages will be prepared in manuscript.

date.	time of parade.	A. Company.	B Company	C. Company	D. Company	Machine Gun Section	Grenades.	Signallers.	Remarks and references to Appendices
3rd	7.0am.	Bayonet drill	Physical drill	Bayonet drill	Physical drill			Physical drill	
	9.30am	Extended order drill	Route march	Extended order drill	Route march			Bayonet practice Lecture on Flavens telephone	
	2.30 pm	Lecture	Lecture	Lecture	Lecture				
4th	7.0am.	Physical drill	Bayonet drill Company drill	Physical drill	Bayonet drill Company drill arms drill	Under Brigade arrangements	Under Brigade arrangements	Physical drill Instruction in use of message form repeater signal	
	9.30am	Route march	Arms drill	Route march				Visual signalling	
	2.30 pm		Arms drill under Battalion Sergeant Major.	Arms drill under Battalion Sergeant Major.					
5th	7.0am	Bayonet drill.	Physical drill.	Bayonet drill	Physical drill.			Physical drill	
	9.30am		Battalion Route march.	Battalion Route march.					
	2.30pm		Foot inspection	Foot inspection					

149th Inf.Bde.
50th Div.

Battn. transferred
to 151st Inf.Bde.
50th Div. 20.12.15.

1/5th BATTN. THE BORDER REGIMENT.

NOVEMBER AND DECEMBER

1 9 1 5

Attached:

Appendices "C" & "D".

D.A.G. 3rd Echelon.

Herewith copy of War Diary of this Bn. for months of Nov: and Dec 1915 and ~~Jan 1916~~. It is regretted that these returns have been delayed.

8/3/16.

J.H.Martin Lt. & Adjt
for O.C. 5/ The Border Regt.

Vol. II
~~III~~
~~IV~~
~~V~~

WAR DIARY or INTELLIGENCE SUMMARY

Army Form C. 2118.

(Erase heading not required.)

Instructions regarding War Diaries and Intelligence Summaries are contained in F.S. Regs., Part II. and the Staff Manual respectively. Title pages will be prepared in manuscript.

Summary of work done for week 6-11-15 to 12-11-15.

Date	Hour	A Company	B Company	C Company	D Company	Remarks and references to Appendices
6th	7am	Physical drill.	Physical drill.	Physical drill.	Physical drill.	M.G. Grenadiers
	9.30am	Extended order drill.	Route march.	Bayonet fighting.	Bayonet fighting.	
	2pm	Lecture on field duties	Lecture on outpost duties	Platoon+Company drill. Lecture on trench duties.	Platoon & Company drill Bayonet practice. Manual (tot. disc)	
7th	7am	Running	Running	Running	Running	
	9.30am					
	2pm		Church Services and Inspections			
8th	7am	Bayonet fighting.	Bayonet fighting.	Bayonet fighting.	Physical drill.	
	9.30am	Route march.	Trenching outposts Route march.	Route march.	Bayonet practice.	
	2pm		Parade under B.S.M. for Arms drill.		disc practice.	
9th	7am	Bayonet fighting.	Physical drill.	Physical drill.	Bayonet fighting.	Under Brigade arrangements
	9.30am		Battalion Route March		Physical drill.	
	2pm		Foot Inspection.			
10th	7am	Physical drill.	Bayonet fighting.	Bayonet fighting.	Bayonet fighting.	
	9.30am	Route march.	Platoon + Company drill extended order drill.	Physical drill open order drill	Arms+section drill	
	2pm	Lecture - outposts.	Lecture on trench duties Lecture-Wiring + Sniping	Lecture- Guard duties.	disc practice.	
11th	7am	Physical drill	Physical drill	Physical drill.	Physical drill	
	9.30am	Trenching outpost work.	Route march.	Route march.	Route march	Under Brigade arrangements.
	2pm		Parade under B.S.M. for Arms drill	Bayonet fighting musketry and fire control		
12th	7am	Bayonet fighting.	Bayonet fighting.	Bayonet fighting.	Physical drill.	
	9.30am	Route march.	Platoon drill Extended order drill.	Open order drill	Route march. Bac. practice.	
	2pm	Lecture- guard duties.	Lecture advance guard rear guard.	Lecture bringing up troops. Lecture.	Lecture Wiring+sniping. Co-op. Coy. practice.	

WAR DIARY
or
INTELLIGENCE SUMMARY.
(Erase heading not required.)

Army Form C. 2118.

Hour, Date, Place	Summary of Events and Information	Remarks and references to Appendices
16th November 1915.	During the period 16th to 28th November, 8 days leave was granted to all the N.C.Os and men who had been in this country since before January 1st 1915 and had not had leave. These amounted to about 340.	
12th November 1915.	During the period 12-11-15 to 19-12-15 similar programmes of work were carried out. Concentration Route marches were arranged by Companies, Battalions and Brigades. Attacks were made on skeleton trenches prepared for the purpose. During the training period 205 men were instructed in the use of bombs and also threw live bombs.	
20th December 1915. 9.30 a.m.	The Battalion moved to huts at DICKEBUSCH and was transferred to the 151st Infantry Brigade, to take the place of the 5th Loyal North Lancs Regt. who had left that Brigade.	
23rd December 1915.	The Battalion took over trenches A.7. to A.12 on the right of HOOGE. The Machine Gun Section is being worked under Brigade arrangement, one section relieving another. LEWIS guns are shortly to be issued to Battalions and one officer (Lt. RHIND) and order have been sent on a Lewis Gun Course.	
24th & 25th December 1915.	The trenches taken over by the Battalion were found to contain a lot of water and much work was necessary to drain them.	
26th December 1915.	Nothing of interest to report. An increase of sniping and in the number of flares sent up by the enemy was noticeable. Training and cleaning trenches was carried on with	
27th December 1915.	Battalion relieved in trenches and proceeded to reserve at SANCTUARY WOOD and CANAL BANK.	

APPENDICES "C" & "D".

5TH BATTALION THE BORDER REGIMENT.

Particulars of Officers.

Officers who came to France 25/10/14.

Lieut.Col. T.A.Milburn.	Invalided to England, 29/7/15.
Major A.C.Scoular.	Invalided to England, 25/5/15.
Major A.D.Soulsby.	Temp. Lieut.Colonel 28/8/15.
Captain A.F.Broadley-Smith.	Temp.Major 18/4/15. Killed in action 16/6/15.
Captain H.J.Bewlay.	Temp.Major 17/6/15.
Captain R.C.R.Blair.	To England (W.O. Special leave) 21/10/15 Rejoined Battalion 2/2/16.
Captain S.Rigg.	To England. 15/9/15.
Captain W.F.Spedding.	To England 5/6/15. Rejd.from England 9/8/15. To England 7/1/16.
Captain H.R.Potts.	To England 26/12/15.
Captain A.B.Cowburn.	
Captain E.A.Iredale.	
Lieut. H.C.Webb.	Temp.Captain 18/4/15. To England 26/5/15. Rejoined Battalion 7/7/15.
Lieut. J.W.Robinson.	Temp.Captain 16/6/15. To England 29/6/15. Rejoined Battalion 7/10/15.
Lieut. W.Adair.	To hospital 22/12/15.
Lieut. W.S.Sewell.	To England 20/5/15. Rejoined Battn. 7/10/15.
Lieut. R.J.Rice.	Temp.Captain 16/6/15. Wounded 5/7/15. To England 22/8/15.
Lieut. F.B.Spedding.	To England 10/2/15.
Lieut.C.N.Jenkins.	To Base duty and struck off strength 22/12/15.
Lieut. F.P.Longmire.	To England 10/5/15.
2/Lieut. C.Graham.	Temp. Lieut. 18/4/15. Killed in action 27/5/15.
2/Lieut. G.G.Askew.	Wounded 6/7/15. To England 15/7/15.
2/Lieut. J.N.Franks.	To England 22/8/15. Rejoined Battalion 1/1/16.

2.

Officers who came to France 25/10/14 (continued)

2/Lieut. H.P.Smith.	Wounded 23/5/15. To England, 27/5/15.
2/Lieut. J.B.McGhie.	To England, 30/4/15. Rejoined Battalion 19/12/15.
2/Lieut. I.H.M.Humphreys.	Wounded 12/6/15. To England 27/6/15.
2/Lieut. P.W.Maclagan.	
Major. & Quartermaster G.Pecker.	To England 13/1/16.
Captain & Adjutant T.W.MacDonald.	To England 26/6/15.
Chaplain & Hon.Lt.Col. Campbell.	To England 27/12/14.
Lieut. W.Marley-Cass, R.A.M.C. Attd.	To England 28/2/15.

Joined 17/12/14.

2/Lieut J.W.Adair.	Wounded 17/5/15. To England 27/5/15.

Joined 9/1/15.

2/Lt. W.F.D. de La Touche.	Wounded 24/5/15. To England 21/7/15.

Joined 12/7/15.

2/Lieut. W.P.Bennett.	Temp. Lieut. 18/7/15.
2/Lieut. H.Bennett.	To England 15/9/15.
2/Lieut. H.E.Wood.	Temp.Lieut. 6/8/15. To 151st Brigade Machine Gun Coy. 6/2/16.
2/Lieut. P.B.C.Holdsworth.	Wounded 14/7/15. To England 23/7/15.
2/Lieut. A.S.Wilson.	Wounded 25/9/15. To England 29/9/15. Rejoined Battalion 31/1/16.
2/Lieut. C.K.Montgomery.	To England 5/12/15.
2/Lieut. D.W.Glass.	a/Adjutant 29/7/15. To duty 12/2/16.
2/Lieut. J.M.Main.	Seconded for duty with 182nd Tunnelling Company, R.E. 2/10/15.
2/Lieut. R.B.Oliver.	
2/Lieut. O.J.Feetham.	
2/Lieut. J.R.Percy.	Wounded 17/7/15. To England 22/7/15. Rejoined Battalion 7/12/15.

Joined 13/7/15.

2/Lieut. R.W.Marley.	Temp.Lieut. 26/6/15. To 151st Brigade Machine Gun Coy. 6/2/16.

3.

Joined 30/7/15.

  2/Lieut. L.Ewbank.   Killed in action 25/2/16.

Commissioned from the ranks.

  2/Lieut. C.E.Pass.   Proceeded to join 2/5th Border Regt. 10/9/15.

Joined 22/9/15, from 5th Royal Berks Regiment as Commanding Officer.

  Major W.R.P.Kemmis-Betty.   To England 26/10/15.

Joined 6/10/15.

  Lieut. G.J.Monson-Fitzjohn.   To R.F.C. and struck off strength 16/1/16

Joined 1/11/15.

  2/Lieut. H.P.Rhind.

Joined 2/11/15.

  2/Lieut. G.Hill.   To England 15/1/16.

Joined 11/11/15, from 6th Bn North'd Fusrs. as Commanding Officer.

  Major J.R.Hedley.

Joined 24/12/15.

  2/Lieut. J.A.Stout.

Joined 8/1/16.

  2/Lieut. G.H.Dawes.

Joined 12/2/16. from The Royal Scots as Adjutant.

  Lieut. J.H.Martin.

Joined 13/2/16.

  2/Lieut. P.Bennett.

Joined 14/2/16.

  2/Lieut. A.L.Ford.

  2/Lieut. A.G.Condi.

APPENDIX 'D'

Officers who have been granted leave to England.

Date	Officers
30th May 1915 to 7th June 1915.	Lieut. Col. J. A. Milburn; Major & Q.M. G. Pecker Capt. R. R. Blair Capt. A. B. Cowburn Lieut. G. G. Askew. Lieut. J. N. Franks.
8th June 1915 to 15th June 1915	Major. A. D. Soulsby Major. A. F. Broadley Smith Capt. & Adjt. J. W. Macdonald Capt. H. R. Potts. Lieut. W. Adair.
7th to 14th July 1915.	Capt. E. A. Iredale.
18th to 24th July 1915.	Lieut. J. B. Spedding. Lieut. P. W. Maclagan.
24th to 31st July 1915.	Capt. M. P. Inglis. R.A.M.C. attd.
30th July to 5th Aug. 1915.	Capt. H. J. Bewlay.
5th to 11th Aug. 1915.	Capt. S. Rigg.
11th to 17th Aug 1915	2 Lieut. C. N. Jenkins.
17th to 23rd Aug. 1915.	Major. G. Pecker.
25th Aug. to 1st Sept. 1915.	Capt. A. B. Cowburn.
31st Aug. to 31st Sept. 1915.	Lieut. Col. A. D. Soulsby
5th to 12th Sept. 1915	Capt. H. R. Potts.
11th to 18th Sept. 1915.	Lieut. J. W. Adair.
24th Sept. to 1st Oct. 1915.	Lieut. P. W. Maclagan.
12th Oct. to 18th Oct. 1915.	Capt. R. R. Blair. D.S.O.
18th to 25th Oct.	Capt. M. P. Inglis Major H. J. Bewlay.
25th Oct. to 1st Nov.	Capt. E. A. Iredale.
31st Oct. to 6th Nov.	Capt. E. A. Iredale
6th Nov. to 12th Nov.	Lieut. W. P. Bennett.

www.ingramcontent.com/pod-product-compliance
Lightning Source LLC
Chambersburg PA
CBHW081449160426
43193CB00013B/2422